UNCLUTTERED
Storage Room by Room

UNCLUTTERED
Storage Room by Room

Candace Ord Manroe

FRIEDMAN/FAIRFAX
PUBLISHERS

A FRIEDMAN/FAIRFAX BOOK

© 1997 by Michael Friedman Publishing Group, Inc.

Library of Congress Cataloging-in-Publication Data available upon request.

ISBN 1-56799-428-8

Editor: Francine Hornberger
Art Director: Jeff Batzli
Designer: Andrea Karman
Layout Designer: Meredith Miller
Photography Editor: Amy Talluto
Production Manager: Camille Lee

Color separations by Colourscan Overseas Co Pte Ltd.
Printed and bound in the USA

1 3 5 7 9 10 8 6 4 2

For bulk purchases and special sales, please contact:
Friedman/Fairfax Publishers
Attention: Sales Department
15 West 26th Street
New York, New York 10010
212/685-6610   FAX 212/685-1307

Visit our website:
http://www.metrobooks.com

To my patient children,
Meagan, Drew, and Sam

C O N T E N T S

Introduction

Making Sense of Your Life

It's no coincidence that our need for better, more efficient household storage increases correspondingly with a technology that's ever more sophisticated. Think about it.

Technology is growing every day, making life a little bit more accessible—and a little less. New gadgets are entering the marketplace each month and streamlining many of life's tasks, but there's an accompanying anxiety: unless one has a mastery of machinery, one will feel a sense of losing control. As the old hands-on approach becomes antiquated by technology, it's hard to feel grounded. This is where good storage comes into play.

Adequate, efficient storage allows you to find the things you need without special computer-age skills. It is a tactile, tangible solution to the complexity of modern society. When good storage is made a priority in your home's design, your life becomes more manageable.

Effective storage helps us to achieve control over our hectic lives. Being immediately able to

Sometimes the best storage solutions allow for the opportunity to display what needs to be stored. Here, an open built-in shelving unit presents a wonderful opportunity to show off a quilter's own handiwork.

put our hands on an insurance policy, a Beethoven CD, or a pair of leather gloves is empowering. Nothing better provides a sense of mastery over life than having easy, ready access to the things we need. Knowing exactly where an old pair of glasses is and being able to retrieve those glasses in seconds may not seem that important, but what a difference something so seemingly trivial can make in your day—the entire scheme of things flows much more smoothly when this kind of efficiency is at your fingertips.

When everything is in its own place, the home becomes a more comfortable place in which to live, a place where you can relax after a long day without being overwhelmed by your possessions. Good storage is truly the secret to living an uncluttered life.

Intelligent storage was a major consideration in the planning of this kitchen and dining room. A multitude of drawers on the kitchen side provides places to stash everything from utensils to napkins. The two-sided cabinets above with access in both rooms have glass doors to display as well as store more formal dishes and art objects.

Function First

One of the precepts of modern design is function before form. The home's design must incorporate adequate storage areas as well as provide appropriate living spaces to meet the owner's needs. No matter how aesthetically pleasing a home or apartment is, if it doesn't meet the needs of its occupants, it's not a design success. More and more people are recognizing this, placing storage at the top of their list of considerations in home design.

This kitchen is blessed with a clutter-free yet decorative appearance. A country table that resembles a desk serves as a kitchen island. The range hood doesn't extend all the way to the ceiling, which creates a niche for shiny pots in various sizes. A wealth of clean white painted cabinets holds everyday dishes, and the window seat not only serves as a place to curl up with a book, but opens at the front to stow any number of things.

Look at photographs in home-decorating magazines. Not so long ago, the functional objects of the household were missing from the dream homes featured on the pages—but not anymore. TVs, phones, CDs, and even the kids' winter coats and scarves are in plain view in even the most upscale domiciles. We're acknowledging the need for homes that not only look good but function well to meet our real, everyday needs. Integrating storage into the home's design is one essential way to ensure that goal. Real-life solutions mean that homes are no longer designed as decorating temples, but as pragmatic responses to how we really live.

Inventive storage solutions alleviate aggravation. When homes are organized with logical storage, basic daily functions demand less time and energy exerted.

Take the time to thoroughly investigate your household storage needs. Not only will you be able to easily find what you need, but you will enjoy the residual benefit of increased mental serenity. When life seems overwhelming, organized storage is one way of regaining a sense of control—and of finding peace.

This book will be your guide to improving the quality of your life through good storage—to living an uncluttered existence. The special

needs of each and every room in your home will be addressed, from public spaces like the entry, living, and family rooms; to rooms designated for food preparation and eating such as the kitchen and dining room; to private spaces like the bedroom and the bath. Also explored are ancillary rooms like the garage, basement, attic, and closets that when properly configured with furniture, built-ins or portables, become dream solutions.

Paint is a valuable tool for creating an uncluttered decor, as demonstrated here. This linen cabinet was painted in a powder-blue hue to blend right into the walls.

CHAPTER ONE

Identifying
Needs

The real work involved in inventing storage solutions for your home isn't a matter of finding the right receptacle. There is an abundance of options available. The most important task you'll need to perform is to identify your storage needs.

Too often we don't spend enough time on this important preliminary step. We may run out and spend money on a storage container when in fact all that was needed was a thorough housecleaning or reorganization. And too often, by failing to properly identify our needs, we end up with the wrong storage solution in the wrong room. By slowing down and getting organized, you can discover storage solutions to last a lifetime.

This chapter will help you embark on finding storage solutions that will work for you. Just remember the following steps: analyze, prioritize, downsize, categorize, scrutinize, visualize, maximize, fantasize. By executing these, an uncluttered life will become a reality.

These cabinets cleverly conceal all kitchen amenities behind glass doors lined with gauzy white curtains, giving the room a sense of openness and keeping clutter to a minimum.

Analyze

Pretend you're a guest or, better yet, an interior designer visiting your home for the first time. It's important to place yourself at this psychological distance in order to be objective. With that attitude in mind, tour your entire home, room by room, with a notepad and pencil in hand. Pay special attention to every closet, as well as to overall room areas. Take into consideration not only what you can see in the room, but what you can't: how efficient is your out-of-sight clothing storage, for example, in dressers and chests of drawers?

Head each page of your notepad with the name of the room, then note everything about the placement and organization of objects in that room that makes you uncomfortable. For example, are videotapes stacked on the floor or on top of the TV in the family room in no

When planning storage for each room in your home, be sure to carefully think out what functions you will be performing in the room, and store items related to that function there. Here, a nighttime reader has built a shelf for books and magazines over the bed.

particular order? Is the entry closet jam-packed with rolls of wrapping paper, ready to topple over when anyone opens the door? Do towels in the linen closet extend too deeply into the recesses of the shelf to be easily retrieved? What about belts, jewelry, and handbags in bedroom closets? Are they messily organized and nonaccessible?

In addition to noticing the placement of things within the room, make sure to also note that everything you need in that room is in fact there and conveniently placed in the area in which it is to be used. To be sure you are considering all functions associated with any given space, mentally walk through a typical day. Think about your routines before and after work and on weekends. If you like to read magazines on the living room sofa, is your magazine collection located within arm's length of the sofa or tucked away in the family room? If you have bathroom readers in your family, is reading material located in that room? Is the phone book stored right by the phone, or is it in a less convenient location? If you usually pay your monthly bills in the living room or the kitchen, are the bills, envelopes, and stamps stored in the same room? If there's something you do in a room, even if only occasionally, the room will function better when it is properly outfitted for that pastime.

Remember again to be honest with yourself about the tasks you perform in a particular room. If you like to indulge in a romance novel late at night in the living room, admit it. Doing so will immediately make you wonder why you're still storing those paperbacks under your bed when you can easily keep them in a small antique trunk right in the living room.

A pristine environment was created in this sparse, warm, all-wood dining room. The antique armoire holds tablecloths, napkins, placemats, and other linens which need only come out during mealtimes. A rag rug softens the hardness of the wood.

Categorize

After taking a storage inventory and downsizing, create sets of similar objects. For example, combine all kitchen textiles in one unit—cloth placemats, napkins, dish towels, and rags can all be stored in the same place. Combining like objects allows you to streamline storage considerably.

Objects don't have to be of the same material (all paper or all textiles) to make sense when grouped together. Determine whether or not there are objects in need of storage that share a similar shape. Belts, ties, and scarves all have a slender shape, for example, so it might make good storage sense to combine them in a single area or container for maximum space efficiency.

Also check over your list to find objects that share a similar function. Outerwear—such as mittens, hats, coats, boots, and galoshes—doesn't need to be stored in more than one area. Is there a solution that allows combining all these items in the same place, perhaps a system of shelving, hangers, and hooks in the entry closet?

A collection of brightly colored glass vases, platters, and art objects are organized with like pieces and stored in this built-in unit with different-sized compartments, creating a useful storage haven as well as a strong design statement in this living room.

Scrutinize

The next part of your storage journey is to evaluate your furniture and already existing storage receptacles. What should stay and what should go will easily be determined once you evaluate your home objectively.

Regard existing furniture with a skeptic's eye. Is each piece meeting your storage needs in an efficient manner? In evaluating a furnishing's storage capacity, look for shelf space, drawers, and cabinet space. Also, consider hidden space potential. A small pedestal table, for example, appears to have no storage potential. But if you skirt the table, you can hide a plastic storage box or stacked containers set underneath.

Jot down the name of each furnishing in your home that seems to be taking up precious space. Then decide if there's any way its lack of storage help can be rectified. You don't have to replace a piece of furniture that isn't storage-worthy, but if budget allows, this can be an option.

Visualize

As you look at your home with an objective eye for storage problems, focus not only on those items that might be better hidden away, but also on those that are clearly meant for exposure. A bedroom or public room may have a vast expanse of open shelving—seemingly a storage solution made in heaven. But is what's stored here unsightly, like an array (or disarray) of assorted papers, ledgers, and envelopes? These items should be concealed behind closed doors. And consider the opposite. Are beautiful objects stored away in a drawer or closed cabinet? Not only objets d'art, but other items, such as textiles associated with handicrafts—colorful spools of thread, skeins of yarn, remnants of fabric—make a compelling composition when massed together in an orderly fashion.

PREPLANNING

To find the storage solution that's right for your room and your lifestyle needs, read architecture and decorating magazines. Because of the variety of styles and tastes reflected in general-interest shelter magazines, chances are good that you'll find a situation that appeals to you.

Start a clip file of these rooms. As your file grows, you'll see certain storage features that the rooms you've collected have in common: built-in storage seating units, sprawling banquettes used as sofas, window seats, discreetly painted overhead shelving, wall-hung cabinetry with furniture situated snugly beneath, symmetrical bookcases on either side of the room's (center) fireplace, or closets stashed demurely in a corner or inconspicuously along an entire wall.

Having determined what you like, it's time to turn to your own home and honestly appraise its possibilities. Before you launch into anything, make a preliminary sketch of your room as it is and another as you want it to be with the added storage features in place. By comparing the sketches you'll be able to ascertain whether or not your plan is viable for your room configuration.

M a x i m i z e

There may be places in your home that offer untapped storage potential. Is there an alcove space beneath the stairs where a closet could be installed? Is the blank wall space in the garage a ready canvas for an array of tools?

You may have more available vertical and horizontal storage space than you think. Walls can be a major storage repository. Are yours being fully utilized with rows of open shelving, pegboards, or cabinets? What about the space above the toilet and sink in the bathroom or above the stove in the kitchen?

Also look underfoot. The floor presents myriad storage opportunities. Except for furniture, what else is taking up valuable space on your floor? In making your inventory, note rooms in which storage containers will add to the decor of your room. Antique boxes and wooden shipping crates would be appropriate in these situations.

Colored straw boxes are perfect, portable receptacles for small odds and ends that loose would be an eyesore—and are lovely items in themselves. Neatly arranged hardcover books and souvenirs from cherished vacations do not ruin the uncluttered scene.

Fantasize

After you've evaluated what's available to you, go back and imagine how, if you were granted a wish list, you might change your rooms to better utilize them. If you had your way, would the guest bedroom be a home office? If so, what would its storage needs be? Don't disregard these dream rooms when you're approaching decisions on storage. Planning now for the future is one sure way to make your dreams come true.

Remember as you plan that because a family's needs and activities are constantly changing, its storage solutions must evolve as well. The storage solutions that worked even a year ago may not work today. And what seems to work today could be useless in a couple of years. Try to forecast change and your family's growth in the coming years, and your storage solutions will follow.

This shelving unit draped with flowing curtains displays books and objets d'art backlit for a dramatic effect in an otherwise sparsely decorated living room.

A Bird's-eye View of Storage Options

Having gone through your home room by room and evaluated all the storage problems, it's time to consider your options to help you in your quest for good storage. Your solution may be as easy as buying portable containers for your goods, or you may need to create a built-in storage unit.

Portables

More than ever before, manufacturers are offering a wide range of storage units made from various materials in all shapes and sizes. While these pieces put function first, some are very stylish. That makes an important differ-ence in providing solutions that help make your home more functional yet conform to your aesthetic standards.

Portable storage containers are designed to be configured to fit your needs. They can be organized vertically or horizontally, and their versatility enables them to be stacked, hung, and put together in any combination.

Where you plan to use a portable storage container will probably be determined by

what material that piece is made of. Wicker baskets and boxes are attractive accents to the home. They can be enlisted as toilet-tissue or towel holders in the bathroom, as magazine or mail caddies, or as kitchen-utensil organizers.

ABOVE: Instead of purchasing a clunky wood or metal filing cabinet to hold papers and such, consider some-thing a little softer. Wicker drawers suspended on an iron frame visually take up less space. OPPOSITE: Colorful round Shaker boxes stacked atop a painted cabinet are great receptacles for a hobbyist's tools.

The basic cardboard box can be used out of sight for any number of items from love notes to socks. Patterned or solid-colored paper boxes offer good looks, an inexpensive price, and a fairly capacious interior. Because they are pretty to look at, they can be left in plain view.

For deeper storage, consider locker-style bins made of wire. A stack of pressed shirts stays fresh and organized in one of these portable containers that can just as easily store a collection of several years' tax returns.

A plastic box allows storage for things you need to see. Videotapes and CDs can be selected at a glance when stored in these stackable units. Special racks designed for housing CDs, audiotapes, and videotapes are worth consideration. These are available in vertical towers or in low-slung varieties when more horizontal space is available in a room.

An important innovation among portable storage units is the modular drawer. Affordable laminated particleboard drawers or plastic wire-style versions are ideal organizers for odds and ends. Stackable drawers can be added to closets or stand alone in the bedroom to accommodate an overflow of clothing

Looking for a clever way to present towels to guests? Try a hand-woven basket lined with the fabric of your choice. In this case, the fabric pattern is picked up from the towels themselves, tying the decor together.

that doesn't fit in traditional bedroom furniture. Fragile garments susceptible to moth damage can be stored in cedar-lined modular drawers or in zip-up garment bags. These zip-up bags are also available in small, compartmentalized versions that can be wall-mounted for housing jewelry.

The accessories that personalize your home can also enhance your home's storage. Beautiful handcrafted Shaker boxes and Nantucket baskets are objets d'art in their own right, but are also prime storage opportunities. Your collection of business cards or stamps can be nicely stored in the Shaker box while picnic silverware can be kept in the Nantucket basket.

Old shipping crates provide display surfaces for collectibles and, more importantly, hideaway storage. Storing kids' schoolwork in shipping crates is an ideal solution for preserving your child's personal history without cluttering your home. When properly cushioned with bubble wrap or soft paper, old milk crates prove an attractive and interesting receptacle for storing an assortment of bud vases. Even the unexpected—a chicken coop or lobster trap—makes for a conversation piece when storing a selection of colorful blankets and quilts or primary-colored children's toys. Be inventive. Just because an object wasn't originally designated for storage doesn't mean you can't enlist it to serve that purpose—with panache.

Special photo boxes, trays for utensil drawers, wire holders for lids to pots and pans, wall-mounted garden tool organizers, and screw-in pantry shelves are also handy solutions that are not only quick and easy to install but quite inexpensive.

Wire closet organizers are available for all your storage needs. Here, a "closet" was created at the end of a hallway by installing a dowel and overhead compartments in what may otherwise have been dead space. Towels and extra blankets are kept in a shelving unit that closes off the space.

Furniture

Not all furniture is created equal when it comes to storage. But even chairs and sofas can maximize their storage potential with beneath-the-seat drawers. A bed can become storage-efficient with a headboard and footboard that include shelf space and display tops. In addition, the bed can be customized with a sliding storage drawer tucked beneath it.

Without question, one of the most functional furnishings in terms of storage are home-entertainment centers. With their long, adjustable shelves and cabinets, they have been specially designed to store electronic equipment, books, art objects, and accessories. Other important storage-oriented furnishings include armoires, trunks, cabinets, and sideboards.

When shopping for furniture, be sure to take your storage needs into consideration. Any furnishing can complement your decor as well as provide a wealth of storage possibilities. Here, an adult-sized "captain's bed" has drawers incorporated into its platform to hold blankets and bulky sweaters.

Architectural Options

Before you spend a dime on a portable storage container or a new furnishing, make sure your home doesn't already offer an opportunity for a quick and easy architectural solution. Bookcases and build-it-yourself entertainment centers are cost-efficient architectural solutions that can streamline storage and add to the architectural interest of your home.

Architectural answers may not be appropriate for the main rooms of your home, but perhaps they are feasible in less finished areas, such as the basement, attic, or garage. Using inexpensive materials like particleboard to add built-ins enables storage to be adapted to a number of rooms—even those with under-the-eaves angles—that don't easily accommodate freestanding furnishings.

Bookcases and home entertainment centers are the most obvious architectural answers, but not the only ones. Consider using banquette seating in your kitchen. The banquette—a diner-style booth—provides under-the-seat storage. In the contemporary living room, the low-slung banquette as a sofa substitute provides an expanse of horizontal storage as well as a clean, crisp look. A bay window in any room is an invitation to add a win-

dow seat with the inherent storage it can provide in the section underneath the seat.

Other opportunities for built-in storage include room corners. In the dining room, these areas are perfect for enclosed or open-shelf storage units. Even the bathtub can be architecturally outfitted with a built-in frame, custom-designed as a storage caddy.

This window seat is not only a welcoming respite for an afternoon cup of tea, but also serves as storage for awkward large-format books. And when the top is lifted on this seat, anything from documents to sheets of music can be carefully tucked away.

CHAPTER TWO

Living Spaces

Your home's "living spaces"—entry, living room, and family room—are the most public spaces in your home and thus should be planned with the intention of giving a good impression to guests. An entry floor strewn with shoes and boots only creates an obstacle to guests who wish to enter. A living room or family room piled to the ceiling with stacks of newspapers, magazines, CDs, videotapes, and other household clutter will not be the ideal space in which to entertain guests. This chapter will tour these rooms and give ideas and suggestions on how to present an uncluttered image to the rest of the world.

The Entry

Starting at the front door, a home reveals just how storage-wise it really is. Even the smallest entry affords storage opportunities for the savvy owner or occupant.

Depending upon the size and points of architectural interest of your entry, it can become a beautifully designed, as well as welcoming, storage haven.

Closet Organization

Most entries include a closet. Does yours spill its contents each time you open the door? Organizing your outerwear seasonally will alleviate the chaos of the entry closet. When it's summer, transfer bulky winter wraps to another place in the home, such as the attic, the basement, or another closet, and leave only light wear—windbreakers, beach coverups, garden shoes, summer hats. Do the reverse when cold weather hits. By alternating the contents, the closet becomes uncluttered and what's in season is immediately accessible.

A mudroom is intended for outerwear and bad-weather necessities like umbrellas. Adding a dowel between the narrow walls also creates a makeshift closet in the room without distracting from the spare decor.

consider storing those in a compartmentalized divider at one side of the closet. If the closet is already chock-full of outerwear, look to available vertical wall space, where recreational gear can be mounted for easy retrieval.

Furniture Solutions

If you have space in your entry for furniture, do not restrict your storage possibilities by bringing in a storage-poor table. It may make an attractive display area for a favorite collectible or objet d'art, but it will do nothing to solve your storage problem. You may consider instead outfitting your entry with a Bombay

Try to keep only outerwear in your entry closet. If this is not feasible, at least limit what's stored here to what is actually used in proximity of the entry. Many options exist in closet dividers that can help you store a number of different things in the same place. For instance, if the entry is where your family looks for sporting goods before an outing,

ABOVE LEFT: When space is available in your foyer, you can make a wonderful impression on guests (and give yourself more storage space) by creating a decorative display of pottery on an antique cabinet. An inexpensive but beautiful urn serves as an umbrella stand in this entry. ABOVE RIGHT: If your home was not configured with an entry closet, don't fret. Chances are your kitchen or another room in your home may have extra space to accommodate outerwear, as in this residence.

chest. It will fit the allocated space and will provide a wealth of storage options inside, as well as a surface to display art objects. Store items like umbrellas, mittens, mufflers, extra sets of car keys, mail, extra vases, or party goods in this chest.

For a larger entry, especially one with above-average ceiling height, consider including an armoire. Antiques or reproductions will add a sense of grandeur to the entrance of the home. You can store attractive, eye-catching goods on top: extra Beacon blankets,

In addition to two ample closets in this entry, storage is provided by a country-style bench with a seat that opens, revealing a secret hiding place. A rack mounted on the wall in the hall between the two closets can hold hats and other outerwear.

Visible storage is appropriate for an entry when items in view are tidily organized and artfully arranged. Pegboard stretched along one wall of the entry makes hanging hats easy—and the hats themselves will become fetching conversation pieces. Hall trees and coatracks don't consume much space and are very convenient—the time that would be spent opening a closet and finding what you need will be eliminated.

colorful quilts, or a surplus of decorative throw pillows. Inside, the armoire provides another space to store clothing outerwear or can substitute as an entry closet in a home that doesn't include one.

If you are set on the idea of having a table in your entry, drape the table with a textile that reaches the floor. An inexpensive sheet topped with a lacy scarf makes a strong design statement. Beneath the skirt you can store a plastic container or cardboard box full of small items.

ABOVE LEFT: A classical urn holds umbrellas in this spacious entry without detracting from the decor. As the entry does not have its own closet, an armoire (as shown in mirror) was commissioned to hold bulky outerwear.
ABOVE RIGHT: This almost all-glass cabinet is on wheels, which makes an otherwise bulky stationary unit conveniently portable.

Living and Family Rooms

The living room can used both formally as the place to entertain guests and informally as the family hangout. A family room may be included in some homes, freeing up the living room for strictly formal use. Whatever the case in your home, storage solutions for the living and family rooms are closely related.

Magazines and books are both common in each room. In addition, both rooms often house electronics equipment—TVs, stereos, perhaps even home theaters. Wet bars with bottles, stemware, and other paraphernalia can be found in either room. Collectibles, toys, and household paperwork can also be

OPPOSITE: This built-in unit carefully conceals household papers and paraphernalia behind its artistically hand-painted doors while shelves that extend from the side hold leather-bound books and pottery. ABOVE: A living room or family room can be a clutter zone, considering all the items that need to be kept there. This clutter-free space contains a compact home-entertainment center for TV, VCR, stereo system, and CDs and videos. A built-in niche on one wall holds collectibles.

found in both. The same storage solutions can be applied whether the room is a casual space or a formal room.

When a single room serves the dual function of family/living room, the abiding function of the space is twofold: to be comfortable enough for family members to relax in yet be sophisticated enough for entertaining guests. At the same time, the room must provide ample storage for the tools of tasks that occur within its walls without disrupting the flow of the interior design. The storage solutions for this room have to be stylish and visually appealing—the plastic wire carts on casters that work for the kitchen, laundry room, or bath will not work here—so that they can enhance the decor of the spaces. Any of the three types of storage alternatives presented in chapter one—portables, hardworking furniture, and architectural built-ins—are applicable in these rooms.

Built-Ins

Usually the home's largest rooms, the living and family rooms afford the most latitude for built-ins. Long walls are obvious sites for permanent shelving, cabinetry, and window seats with below-surface storage. Given enough

ABOVE: Sparse and elegant, this living room maintains its appearance thanks to two large closets that flank the fireplace. Painted white with no-nonsense knobs, they blend right into the minimalist-inspired decor. OPPOSITE: The rustic integrity of this lodge-like living room is enhanced by wooden bookshelves built almost to the barreled, log ceiling.

depth, a public room can even be outfitted with an entire wall of closets. Attractive louvered closet doors painted to match the walls can virtually "disappear" into the room's decor.

A quick glance at your room will tell you if it's a likely candidate for the addition of built-ins. If the room is cramped, anything added to the walls that cuts into floor space will obviously be more of a detriment than an asset. Also, if walls are odd, asymmetrical sizes, the addition of architecture may throw off the room's balance. If the walls are covered with windows, available wall space will probably be too limited to make built-ins viable.

Sometimes, however, built-ins are exactly what a room needs to complete its decor. For example, if the room has a center fireplace, adding built-ins on either side will create a wonderfully symmetrical, balanced space. A long wall in a room is also a contender for an architectural answer. And if necessary furniture is already lined up on the wall, adding built-in storage areas is still possible. Just build permanent bookcases, shelves, or

The storage needs of this family room are addressed by both open and closed options in one unit. On top, the stereo is easily accessible and books are displayed. Below, board games, CDs, and other family entertainment activities are stowed.

cabinetry over the height of the furniture. Lightweight furniture can even be flanked against cabinets that are built to store objects that aren't needed often.

Does one wall of your room include a centrally placed window? If so, consider adding a window seat underneath, stretching not only under the window but along the entire length of the wall. A window seat can be a cozy place for curling up with a book, and its long reach

across the wall ensures ample hidden storage below its bench seat. Sliding cabinet doors on the lower portion allow contents to be both stored out of sight and easily retrieved. While the most common decorating treatment is to paint the lower section the same color as the room's walls or the same color as its accent trim, a bolder decorative paint treatment— perhaps a trompe l'oeil scene depicting clouds, an English garden, ancient ruins, or

The high ceiling in this sparse loft space allows room for an extensive shelving system that provides more storage than is needed for the easy growth of an already-abundant library.

d'art. Because you are in charge of the configuration, each inch can be utilized wisely.

Your built-in can be given a stronger architectural presence by adding a decorative molding to hide the seams. Whether your space is a contemporary family room or a traditional living room, there is a decorative molding available to blend harmoniously with your room's design style.

Consider the Consequences

Before embarking on an architectural solution, be sure to consider how you may feel about living in a construction zone. Knocking down walls and recontouring them is a major undertaking and will demand patience and flexibility from your entire family.

Most importantly, think about your budget constraints. This undertaking can be an investment whether you do it yourself or hire professionals. Even if the addition isn't cost-prohibitive, it may require more of an investment in your home than you're willing to make. If you will not be living in your present home for more than a few years, perhaps you should investigate another storage option.

But dealing with built-ins doesn't have to be such a complicated matter. You certainly don't have to knock down walls or drain your

anything you find appealing—will make it a striking pièce de résistance.

Adding shelves yourself enables you to customize the placement, leaving greater distances between shelves when needed for tall books or collectibles, and less for smaller items. You may opt to enclose some of the shelves (it usually makes sense to do this with the lower section only) with sliding or pull-open doors. Your shelving unit can be designed and constructed to fit your every need with tiny pockets for CDs and videos or niches for sculptures or other favorite objets

This room remains clutter-free thanks to two cleverly built-in receptacles: a window seat under a bright arched window and a shelving and cabinet unit.

bank account to create them. On a more modest scale, built-ins can be added that aren't disruptive to daily living while being installed. Investigate those that require little expertise and can be done by yourself so that you can stay within a conservative budget.

Display and Hideaway Storage

Once you've decided to create built-in storage in your living room or family room, you need to establish what you're going to store there and whether it merits being out in the open or behind closed doors. A cache of colorful kid's toys with their brilliant primary colors and distinct geometrical shapes can create an interesting display. And if toys are left out in

the open, children will have easier access to them. On the other hand, old papers, letters, ledgers, and the like that are not visually appealing or don't need to be easily accessible are best stored behind a closed door.

Closet Storage

Another alternative is to build into the closet in these rooms or to add a closet if none exists. Given enough depth in the public room, adding roomy storage behind sliding closet doors that blend unobtrusively with the walls is worth considering. Louvered doors painted the same color of the walls are inconspicuous. Or you can call attention to the doors as more of a focal point or item of visual interest with a decorative paint treatment. Unusual building materials, such as custom twig slats or

Now you see it, now you don't. What seems to be an elegant but ordinary wood-inlaid wall is really a wall of closets that opens up to reveal a TV, stereo, and wet bar. When these are not in use, the wall becomes a plain surface again.

Or, cover the TV shelving unit with a fabric-covered shade or matchstick blind typically used for a window treatment. This adds a decorative element to the living space while hiding the equipment. You may want to build shelves for your TV equipment behind a sliding wood panel mounted on a rod. This sliding panel can be covered in fabric, painted the color of the room, or turned into a work of art with an original painting. You can mount art from your existing collection onto the panel, treating it more as a wall than as a door.

beautifully colored and patterned fabric panels, will add textural interest to the room.

What will be stored in the closet will determine how the interior is outfitted. A portable-container system may be used to efficiently organize items in a modular configuration that's arranged to fit the goods exactly. Another option is to hang easy do-it-yourself shelves for linear storage with a clean, streamlined look.

Out-of-sight materials can be stored in your closet, but what about items that you sometimes want exposed, and then concealed when not in use, like the TV? Especially in a formal living room, a TV can be disruptive to the feel of the space. Why not keep your TV on a rolling cart inside your closet?

ABOVE LEFT: A delightful collection of miniature chairs can be shown off for company and then protected from dust behind the doors of this large cabinet. ABOVE RIGHT: This beautiful wood armoire displays a collection of pottery and blends right into the decor when the doors are closed. The end table is made of a wicker basket filled to the top with hardcover books and a painted wood box that can stash magazines and paperbacks.

Room Dividers

A room divider can also increase the storage possibilities in your living or family room. For an open feel in the space, build your divider at waist height, preserving the visual continuity between either side of the divider. If you want to delineate a clearer boundary between areas of the room and provide a sense of privacy between spaces, build your divider from ceiling to floor.

As with other built-ins, the storage divider can be outfitted with either open shelving or cabinetry on both sides. Display books, collectibles, plants, or other objects you don't mind keeping exposed on shelves, and put less attractive materials behind closed doors.

Banquette Seating

The sofa is typically the living or family room's most space-guzzling furnishing and has virtually no storage potential. Try banquette seating in your room instead. Easy to construct, this architectural alternative simply follows the contours of the wall, like a window seat, but with deeper, more comfortable proportions. And there's no rule that the banquette must be wall-bound. It can be built anywhere in the room, provided that the owner has

taken care to ensure that a middle-of-the-room location is exactly the one desired—once it's put there, there it will stay.

Outfit banquette seating with lush tapestry throw pillows to create a traditional feel. Keep in mind that this seating option is especially compatible with contemporary room designs because of its streamlined form. The storage

A room divider as well as a clever storage solution, this curved unit, made of laminate that matches the white starkness of the rooms it separates, holds books on one side, dishware on the other. A fish tank has also been included in the configuration.

solution afforded by the banquette occurs in its lower reaches. Designed with below-the-seat storage drawers or cabinets, the banquette puts the space left idle by the sofa to use for storage.

Making Furniture Functional

Less costly and troublesome than adding architecture to a room is to purchase storage-conscious furniture. Too often, furniture decisions are made solely on the basis of what looks and feels good—the storage function may not even be considered. But if you consider the storage possibilities of furnishings before you purchase them, you'll end up with something that's not only visually pleasing but useful as well. Case goods can be found in virtually every type of furniture and are available in diverse styles and prices.

What purpose does the vacant area beneath your glass-topped cocktail table serve? Why not put it to storage use? More and more major furniture manufacturers are offering attractive cocktail tables equipped with drawers or cabinets for hidden storage. Often, these same pieces include a shadow-box top that provides a roomy, protected-under-glass display area for small collectibles. End tables can provide more than just a top

surface for lamps and accessories. A sensible trade-off for a table with showy legs is one with a closed-up or shelved lower section that provides excellent storage space for remote controls, paperbacks, and magazines.

If your sofa is not flush with the wall, add a sofa table behind it that includes cabinetry. This furnishing takes up no more space than

OPPOSITE: This room serves double duty as a living room and a family room. During family time, the doors of this cabinet and room divider open to reveal the TV, but when company's over, the doors are closed, providing a sleek environment for entertaining. ABOVE: A unit built up to the ceiling stores books and art objects, as well as a TV. A prized book open to a favorite illustration resting on a wrought-iron stand is a decoration in itself.

an open-legged version, while offering storage that runs the length of the sofa itself.

Trunks, boxes, and shipping crates are designed for storage but can become furnishings within themselves. The old trunk from your grandmother's attic makes a highly functional TV stand or coffee table while providing hidden storage for off-season clothing or keepsakes. Wicker boxes or old toolboxes can store magazines or toys, and when set beside a chair can also become small tables. Stacked one atop the other, a collection of decorative boxes makes an artful furnishing.

Don't forget old wooden shipping crates. These can come in handy for stashing years of kids' schoolwork while their tops can be adorned with a display of collectibles, a lamp, or perhaps a TV. Larger versions may serve as a conversation-piece cocktail table. An old wire-sided chicken coop or lobster trap

A straw trunk is a delightful accent in this living room and serves more than one purpose. Foremost, it assumes the role of a coffee table, but it has the added bonus of being able to hide away anything from an extra blanket to board games to playing cards.

home and emphasizes a natural palette and organic materials is natural linen. Adding textural interest to the home, linen-cloaked organizers look more like furniture than portable containers.

Clear plastic tubs and boxes, wire bins and baskets, and other related inexpensive containers may not add high-style looks to a living or family room's interior-design scheme, but you would be amazed at how much they can improve the space's appearance by organizing clutter. If the rest of the room is well-designed for a strong aesthetic statement, its integrity won't be too threatened by a few storage containers in plain view.

turned cocktail table stores multifarious quilts or blankets—or a collection of carved hens or decoys—with wry wit.

Portable Solutions

When budget or space constraints don't permit adding architecture or buying furniture, portable organizers can come to the rescue. As addressed in chapter one, there are a number of options available. One of the freshest looks in these small containers that is perfect for the

ABOVE LEFT: This unit is chock full of plastic boxes originally intended for food storage. Here, they are labeled to contain children's toys and collected treasures like seashells and rocks. ABOVE RIGHT: Children's toys and books can be at home in the family room through careful planning and organization. This corner space set off from the rest of the room is a playroom in itself. A short shelf keeps books and toys within easy reach of small arms.

CHAPTER THREE

The Kitchen and the Dining Room

The dining room is usually a formal area where family meals are served and is usually located in close proximity to the kitchen. Precise functions between these rooms differ, but there is overlap. The eat-in kitchen can serve the dining function and in some cases is the formal dining space. Therefore, the storage needs of both spaces can be viewed alongside each other, as many of the accouterments associated with dining can be stored in both spaces.

Decide which items are used most often in which space. Are lace table linens used only in the formal dining space? If so, store them only in that room. Reserve storage space in the kitchen for the everyday table dressings—napkins, place mats, and tablecloths. The same applies to tableware—stemware, flatware, china, vases, table centerpieces, and other accessories. If the good silver is used exclusively in the formal dining room, store it there. When flatware is used interchangeably between the kitchen eating area and formal dining room, determine the spot where your family dines most frequently and keep the flatware there.

These side-opening drawers ingeniously solve the problem introduced by the angled counter in this space-efficient kitchen.

The Kitchen

Without much debate, the kitchen is the most functional room in the home, and thus the one with the greatest storage requirements. The amount of storage space a kitchen has to offer can sometimes be a determining factor in a new home purchase.

The importance of kitchen storage is also illustrated by the rising number of professional kitchen designers. These specialists are hired

to utilize every available inch of possible storage space. Today's luxury kitchen doesn't boast only state-of-the-art appliances and the finest building materials, the ingredient that distinguishes the dream kitchen is innovative storage solutions.

ABOVE LEFT: Shelves that pull out from behind closed doors provide the convenience of access to any pot or pan the chef desires without the hassle of burrowing into the far reaches of a low-ceilinged cabinet. ABOVE RIGHT: This kitchen also takes into account the convenience that slide-out shelves provide. What might have been an obtrusive addition to the limited counter space here, a professional-sized mixer is stowed away in a cabinet with a shelf that pulls out to provide a place to use the piece.

ware, cabinetry that includes a combination of open shelves for the most frequently used items plus glass-door cabinets to allow pretty kitchenware to be viewed. Lower cabinets are actually deep rollout trays sized for pots and pans, with sectionals to keep things neat. A smaller, separate drawer is also sectionalized to accommodate lids, organizing them individually for easy retrieval. Special small drawers stacked closely together are designed just for spices. Pantry shelves swing out for easy accessibility. Fresh produce is stored in built-in wire-basket vegetable bins. The ends of counters may also be outfitted with deep

A Dream Kitchen

The dream kitchen provides a place for everything. Some features may include a metal-lined bread drawer (no more cluttering the countertops with a freestanding bread box—or, worse still, stashing the bread on top of the refrigerator), sectionalized drawers for flat-

ABOVE LEFT: The pyramid design of this over-the-counter shelving unit gives this warm-toned kitchen added visual interest. It makes a convenient receptacle for baskets and pitchers too lovely to lock away in a closet.
ABOVE RIGHT: A contemporary portable wire cart on casters with pull-out drawers to the left tucks away kitchen essentials while providing a butcher-block top surface—an ideal workspace. A traditional wrought-iron baker's rack on the other side of the stove is an attractive and accessible receptacle for pots and pot holders.

drawers for storing onions, potatoes, and other longer-life perishables. There is a built-in storage space for the wastebasket, another for recyclables, and yet another for refundable beverage containers.

Planning by Function

Placement of specialized storage features is just as important as their presence. Kitchen designers understand that accessibility means everything to the hurried home chef. With lit-tle time to waste, it's essential that the kitchen be designed to offer the items needed at the homeowner's fingertips. Extra steps need to be eliminated: simply by stretching out a hand, the homeowner should be able to obtain any items needed for the task at hand. This means organizing the kitchen into task areas: a bake center, food preparation center (a primary and auxiliary prep center are included in the most spacious kitchens), cleanup center, and so on.

The cleanup center should place the dish-washer and sink near one another, and should

Sleek and streamlined, this well-organized kitchen is divided into three distinct sections: food preparation, cooking, and clean up. The convenience of having everything accessible in its respective workspace makes an uncluttered lifestyle a reality.

call a cabinet manufacturer for a free brochure. This will enable you to identify the cutting-edge storage features available today in kitchen cabinetry.

Open Kitchen Storage

Is there a surface available in your kitchen that can display everyday utilitarian pieces as objets d'art? If your cabinet tops don't extend all the way to the ceiling, you can turn that dead space into a display shelf.

When cabinets flank a window, transform the cabinet sides into corner shelves for collectibles. By mounting small shelves, either

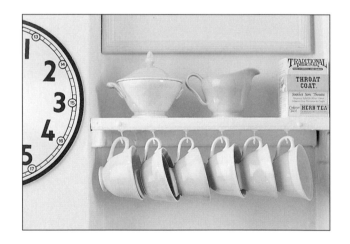

also have nearby storage areas for detergents, sponges, dish rags, and towels, as well as waste receptacles. In the bake center, storage for long, skinny cookie trays, cumbersome cake pans, glass pie pans, and other special baking cookware as well as hot pads and wire cooling racks should be considered. The food preparation center should include storage space for a cork-bottom knife drawer or shelf, as well as space for colanders, vegetable scrub brushes and peelers, and the like.

Home-decorating magazines produce special kitchen issues on dealing with kitchen storage, so peruse these regularly. You can also

square-shaped or with rounded fronts, into the outermost edges of the cabinets between the cabinets and windows, you have utilized dead

ABOVE LEFT: The island is the ubiquitous design element for the modern kitchen. They are available in a variety of shapes and sizes and can be built into the kitchen or added later—there is a model available for every kitchen user's needs. In a spacious kitchen such as this, a built-in island in the same warm palette of the room serves many purposes. It is a workstation, an eating place, and has a wellspring of shelves for storage. ABOVE RIGHT: Teacups in pastel colors suspended from hooks under a small shelf that holds the sugar and creamer are playful decorative accents in this retro kitchen.

the kitchen with a cheery focal point. A painted shelf fits nicely over a short window for display purposes.

For a large collection of attractive or collectible kitchen dinnerware that can't be accommodated in one of the earlier solutions, consider adding a single shelf about eighteen inches (46cm) below the ceiling to run the perimeter of the walls. This solution draws the eye upward and visually makes the kitchen a whole. Adorned with a splashy array of china plates, the shelf's primary function as storage is all but forgotten by its dynamic design statement.

The sides of kitchen islands are another opportunity for open storage. If they are not utilized for appliances or dining space, the sides can easily be outfitted with shelves to house anything from extra salt and pepper shakers to a set of brandy glasses.

But shelving is only one way to provide viewable storage. Kitchens that are large enough to house freestanding furnishings in addition to wall-mounted cabinetry can include an open-faced cupboard or china cabinet to augment the room's built-in storage. These pieces work best when the goods stored within them are of the same type or are in some way visually related. A collection of pitchers, for example, may feature different

space and provided an opportunity to store goods and add character to your kitchen.

What about the area between hanging cabinets and the counter's backsplash? Is there room for pegboard or for individually mounted hooks? Hang your most attractive coffee mugs or china cups here. Cups are organized in an easily retrieved grouping that provides

Adding shelving around the perimeter of the room was the best possible storage solution for this period kitchen. The top portion displays gleaming copper cookware. Below, porcelain containers and pitchers are held. Stemware hangs from the bottom of the next shelf that provides a place for glassware and a clock. Dishes are stored in cylindrical baker's racks, eliminating the need for cabinets.

be out of place. These furnishings provide a light, airy look as is found in some European-country designs, and they offer practical storage solutions.

Enclosed Kitchen Storage

In deciding on a closed storage furnishing, determine whether you'll regret not being able to display your stored goods for all to see. Also base your decision on a realistic appraisal of your neatness: if you know that openly stored pieces, no matter how visually pleasing, will end up in a state of disarray, opt for hidden storage.

patterns or shapes, but visual harmony abides from the similarity of their shapes and their single function. Care should be taken to keep the items in these furnishings tidily arranged; otherwise, the clean look that good storage can provide won't occur.

Baker's racks and étagères make great open-storage furniture for kitchens. Often crafted of iron or another metal, these furnishings are especially desirable for a contemporary or eclectic kitchen design in which a solid-wood case good with a dark grain would

ABOVE LEFT: An ingenious design, between mealtimes this eating station folds up into the cabinets, making the space seem more spare and roomy. A mirror under the glass-faced cabinets visually extends the space. ABOVE RIGHT: Glass-paned cabinet doors in the kitchen help eliminate clutter while giving the space a more open appearance. The island also helps to store kitchenware.

Shelving can be adapted with lift-up, pull-open, or sliding doors to hide stored contents. But expanding the shelving concept to closed-door cabinetry is not recommended for shelves mounted high onto walls. Imagine how a kitchen can become obscured with the visual block of an enclosed cabinet above a window: this closed-door storage would stop the eye at the cabinet doors instead of allowing it to roam all the way to the wall, and would thus cut off perceived square footage. It is truly important to weigh how this will affect the room as a whole before opting for this type of storage.

The charm of a country-style blue-and-white kitchen is heightened by the addition of two long shelves covered with scalloped fabric over a closed cabinetry unit that also serves as a workstation. Delightful accents such as ceramic canisters and pitchers only add to the look. An interesting solution, a tiered unit of baskets holds a variety of breads.

Portable Answers

While most homeowners find it impractical to gut their existing kitchen and replace it with an entirely new one, it's possible to improve storage conditions relatively inexpensively within an existing kitchen. Portable organizers for drawers, cabinets, and pantry closets ensure great storage possibilities for little expense. Any kitchen store or mail-order kitchen catalog as well as retail stores and general storage catalogs will provide what you need. Here are a few places that can benefit from portable storage solutions.

Cabinets

If you have a large cabinet space beneath the sink, allow just enough room for the wastebasket, then mount a wire shelf above it for shorter objects such as sponges, wire brushes, and other food-preparation or cleanup items. Wire racks suspended on the inside of the cabinet door create organized storage space for taller detergents and cleaning products. Because the below-sink cabinet is deep, the space occupied by the door-mounted rack's depth won't interfere with the wastebasket. Do be sure, however, that the shelf attached above the wastebasket is mounted far enough onto the rear of the cabinet to allow room for the door shelves.

Replace the shelves in your pots-and-pans cabinet with a couple of revolving, spin-out, plastic-covered wire racks. These allow each pot and pan its own space without cumbersome stacking. The revolving feature also eliminates the time-consuming task of excavating the cabinet to retrieve the desired item. Designate a portion of the cabinet to hang vertical plastic-coated wire racks that organize pan lids. Save space for similar wire racks that are taller than those for lids. With close-together compartments, these portable organizers allow cookie sheets, pizza pans, and muffin pans to be individually stored on their sides.

This oak taboret serves more than one purpose: it is a receptacle for everyday dinnerware and a work surface when the top doors are shut. A niche under shelves constructed from the same wood provides a home for the unit when it's not in use.

Measure your kitchenwares and plan accordingly. You may outfit a cabinet with more or differently spaced shelves and then organize those shelves further with vertically placed shelf dividers that create cubbyholes for special items. This solution not only eliminates your searching time, it protects breakables by segregating them into their own area. For example, by breaking up a fourteen-inch (35.5cm) cabinet into shelving units of only a couple of inches each, dinnerware can be stored efficiently with minimal breakage and chipping resulting from stacking.

Drawers

Drawers are wonderful receptacles for smaller kitchen items, and with the help of store-bought organizers, will help to optimize your kitchen's storage potential.

Many organizers specially designed for cutlery and flatware are available today and made from materials in anything from wood to plastic to straw, and come in a variety of sizes to fit any drawer.

One of the most innovative and interesting drawer organizers is one that arranges spices in rows for the depth of the drawer. This

ABOVE LEFT: Canned and dry food and dishware may not be the only things you'll want to store behind closed doors in your kitchen. This specially adapted piesafe includes an enclosed shelf for a microwave. If you plan to do this, be sure there is ample room in the compartment for ventilation, as well as a place for wire to go through. ABOVE RIGHT: Portable wire racks have revolutionized kitchen storage, especially in the case of lids for pots and pans. They are usually configured to hold a variety of sizes, as demonstrated here.

invention eliminates the need for a separate spice rack that can take up precious counter or wall space and keeps spices within easy reach of the chef.

Pantry and Broom Closet

Kitchen closets can be reconfigured with portable organizers in much the same way as cabinets. To determine shelf heights, start at the bottom, putting your heaviest, largest canned goods here. Plan enough vertical space to accommodate these items. Locate the next shelf at the corresponding height and plan to store lighter-weight dry goods here.

Proceed upward, putting your smallest and lightest items at the top of the closet.

Don't limit shelf placement to the interior of the closet. The inside of the closet door can be outfitted with narrow, build-it-yourself wood shelves or wall-mounted wire racks to house an overflow of canned goods, vitamins, cooking oils, and other small items.

For the floor space within the closet, think about including stackable pullout bins or drawers, or small portable carts on casters. Large bags of pet food, litter, or any family-size products can be handily accessed from one of these rollout containers.

ABOVE LEFT: Carefully planned and sectioned drawers make cooking easy in this efficient kitchen. A top drawer has been partitioned off to separate kitchen gadgets while the bottom drawer holds a rack for spices, seasonings, and sauces within easy reach of the family chef. ABOVE RIGHT: An ingenious solution, this pull-out cabinet was designed to hold recyclables in order to avoid having too many trash receptacles out in the open. Cans, paper, and plastic, as well as dry dog food are stored here. OPPOSITE: A pantry can be configured to hold any number of items in your kitchen, from canned and dry goods to a mop and broom to dishware. A frosted glass door on this pantry conceals clutter within while visually opening the space.

Countertops

In the disorganized kitchen, countertops can overflow with clutter. But unless cupboard space is extremely capacious, it's not realistic to imagine the opposite extreme where a counter exists entirely free of objects. In between is a reasonable approach to storage, and portable organizers are the answer.

Portable organizers for the countertop aren't a new invention: canisters for flour, sugar, and other staples have been fixtures in the home for generations. But as our food options have increased, so have the number of containers for storing food.

Many families keep several varieties of rice on hand for cuisines from Chinese to Italian. Once the package is opened, storing the unused portion back in the pantry is a nuisance, requiring plastic baggies, rubber bands, or some other makeshift solution to prevent

Your walls are invaluable resources for freeing up countertops from clutter. Here, canisters and spices as well as knives are kept off the counter but in arm's reach of the chef in their own specially configured spots.

frequently (which should be what you keep most accessible) is also among your best-looking.

Walls

Walls don't have to be outfitted with finished shelving to provide storage. Wall-mounted plastic-covered wire racks in all shapes and sizes can house a plethora of kitchen items. Several containers can be grouped together on a wall to avoid the potential visual imbalance that a single, small container by itself can

spillage and bug infestation. See-through plastic jars with tight-fitting lids, however, protect the rice and allow it to be stored directly on the countertop. Pasta varieties are also increasingly popular and can add to the ambience of the kitchen when organized in tall transparent jars or bottles atop the counter.

Plate racks and cutlery holders also provide on-the-counter storage when cabinet and drawer space is limited. For this open storage, it's a bonus if the dinnerware you use most

ABOVE LEFT: Taking advantage of unused space over the range hood, this shelving unit provides storage for everything from cooking oils and roasting pans to cereal. ABOVE RIGHT: Instead of hiding heirloom china in a hutch in the dining room, the owners of this narrow kitchen opted to build a U-shaped shelving system over the stove and countertop to create a lovely display.

sometimes create. Everything from vitamins to spices can find a home in one of these inexpensive wall shelves.

Ceilings

Don't forget to look up when considering storage for pots and pans as well as small quanti-

ties of produce. Ceiling-mounted racks allow your gleaming copper or professional-quality pots and pans to be admired by all—and to become attainable with no bending and searching. Tiered wire mesh baskets hung from the ceiling are ideal for storing colorful produce.

ABOVE LEFT: The wall next to the cooking station in this kitchen was outfitted with hooks to hold everything from salad tongs to meat forks to oversize ladles. Spices and seasonings are contained in specially configured shelves. Wooden spoons are held in their own easily accesible compartment. ABOVE RIGHT: Hanging pots from the ceiling makes them easy to get at as well as makes a strong design statement.

The Dining Room

Handsome dinnerware is most easily displayed in the formal dining room. Here, fewer objects require storage than in the kitchen and those selected for open-storage display serve not only to enhance the room's character, but to function as art.

One of the most pleasing areas for creating open storage is in the corners of the room. Ideally, the wall chosen has a center window or a bank of several windows bisecting the wall. Storage shelves placed on either corner of the wall create a symmetrical balance with the

A built-in hutch maximizes this dining room's square footage because it affords space that may have been taken up by a freestanding unit. China and art objects are stored on open shelves while pull-out drawers below hold table linens and other dining accessories.

windows, adding a finished look to the overall room and calling attention to the windowed wall as a focal point. These shelves are easy to make and to install and are inexpensive—they are mostly made from wood and paint. They also recall older homes in which built-in corner cupboards or shelves were a common architectural feature for the dining room.

To blend well with the room, the shelves should be painted the color of the architectural trim used throughout the space. Bright white shelves against a papered or fabric-covered wall will tie in to a room's white moldings and the trim around windows and doors, for example.

The dining room can benefit from open storage created by hanging a single wood shelf around the perimeter of the space. This storage is recommended only for households that have a large single collection of dinnerware or a collection of different patterns in related motifs and colors. A display of Blue Willow and Blue Danube china patterns, for instance, can be stored together on the shelf without creating a discordant effect. But a soft pastel pattern

An antique hutch stores a collection of porcelain pitchers and serving bowls in this beautifully stenciled dining room. During mealtimes, the hutch can be closed.

styles, from eighteenth-century traditional antiques to natural-look whitewashed furnishings to sleek, lacquered contemporary pieces, with a supply of painted or primitive country offerings in between. Don't fill precious square footage with consoles or side tables that present only a tabletop surface for displaying objects. Consider instead using a cabinet or china hutch to address your storage needs as well as provide a showcase. Baker's racks are also worth considering if their breezy, informal style works with the overall mood of your dining room.

displayed with a contemporary motif in bright primary colors will create a jarring effect, giving the room a sense of clutteredness.

Shelves can be fitted under chair-rail moldings in your dining room. Best situated on one of the room's narrow walls for an unobtrusive fit, shelves that run from the chair-rail to the floor add to the architectural richness of the room. In addition to serving as a storage repository for dinnerware, these shelves can accommodate an overflow of buffet items or serving pieces during a dinner party.

Dining room furnishings are made for viewable storage. Whether constructed with glass doors or open shelving, an array of china cabinets and cupboards are available in all

ABOVE LEFT: The unfinished wood shelving unit complements the painted kitchen chairs and table and picks up on the room's decidedly country feel while at the same time stores dishes, baskets, and a playful rooster-shaped cookie jar. ABOVE RIGHT: Open built-in shelving in this formal dining room displays a treasured collection of serving pieces. The cabinet below holds more practical items.

CHAPTER FOUR

The Bathroom

The bathroom demands hardworking storage solutions. If a pristine nary-an-object-in-sight appearance is the goal for your bath, storage must be addressed in the design. With inventive hidden storage in cabinets and closets as well as less expected places, it is possible to achieve a sparse, clutter-free look. And because most people will settle for a slightly more lived-in look, a number of options in open storage exist that can transform the smallest bathroom into a utilitarian work space.

The two most important steps you can take to good bathroom storage are downsizing and categorizing. After you've tackled these, you may be surprised how little you actually have left to store in your bathroom.

D o w n s i z e

There's no question: the bathroom is always one of the most cluttered rooms in the home. Before you're even aware of a problem, long-forgotten bottles of nail polish, aftershave, colognes, hairspray, and face-cleaners become stockpiled.

With a garbage bag in tow, examine products stored in the bathroom. Are those extra, nearly empty tubes of toothpaste ever really going to be the lifesaver you saved them for? How many extra toothbrushes are necessary? If you don't like the face-cleansing products you bought last year, why assume you'll wake up one morning with a change of heart? Trash them (or give them to a friend, who may have a better appreciation). Exhibit the same ruthlessness with old makeup. It's easier to admit you bought the wrong lipstick and throw it away than it is to store it.

Pay special attention to prescription and over-the-counter drugs: they don't keep forever. Go through your collection and toss each drug that has expired. Get into the habit of regularly checking this shelf. You'll be maintaining up-to-date pharmaceuticals and improving your storage at the same time.

If you're like most homeowners, staying uncluttered in the bathroom isn't just a matter of staying on top of the accumulation of small items. You probably have extra bath towels hanging around that may have lost their newness and are ready for the "rag bag." A regular check of your towels' condition will keep your stack from mounting too high—and will allow you to make your best impression on guests.

C a t e g o r i z e

Providing tidy, well-organized storage in the bathroom is a real challenge. Even in the most efficient households, cleaning products and toiletries tend to stray from one contained area into several different locations, making retrieval time-consuming and frustrating.

Group all paper goods in one area, below the sink or in an upper cabinet, and all shaving paraphernalia in another. Bath soaps, body exfoliates, and bath beads can be stored in yet another area. In addition to improving storage in your bath area with a thorough cleanup, this simple organization will not only make items more accessible but presentable.

The best way to eliminate clutter in the bathroom is to throw away items you don't need. Toiletries can be taken out of their bulky boxes and stored in glass canisters on a decorative tray, as shown here.

Portable Solutions

Organize items into discreet sets with trays, jars, bottles, boxes, baskets, and stackable tubs—small containers that fit easily on top of a counter or within a drawer or cabinet. Cotton balls, for example, are much handier when put in a glass or plastic jar, eliminating the awkward paper or plastic bag in which they are sold. Q-Tips fit neatly into a glass canister or bottle, reducing retrieval time while creating a less cluttered space. These receptacles can be stored directly on the vanity or any countertop or table surface. They can be hidden in a medicine cabinet or behind closet doors. The receptacles improve organization, even when the storage is concealed.

Display hair products together on a tray. Although this doesn't actually reduce the number of items, it makes them look

ABOVE LEFT: This ornately carved Asian-inspired wood shelving unit may at first seem incongruous, but it works nicely within the decor of this bath. Not only does it serve the functional purpose of accommodating towels and toiletries, it gives the room an added sense of design. ABOVE RIGHT: Relatively inexpensive at home stores and five-and-dime outlets, wire carts on casters are perfect for bathrooms as they are sturdy and mobile, and can hold a number of things from towels to sponges and bath oils.

presentable. Trays come to the rescue not only for grouping toiletry items that are displayed in the open, but work equally well inside drawers. Small, compartmentalized plastic trays take the mishmash out of a catch-all drawer—hair ribbons, scrunchies, and barrettes in one area of the tray, razor blades and shaving brush in another. Trays are especially good for organizing drawers, as their dimensions lend themselves to the shallow depth of a drawer space.

Woven baskets and decorative wooden boxes are wonderful organizers for bathroom items, and their appearance adds texture and warmth to the room. Small versions fit directly onto vanities or tables, holding everything from tissues to matchbooks. Although your bathroom may include adequate storage for linens in closets or cabinets, consider keeping a fresh supply of hand towels in a small basket. House guests will be thankful.

Larger baskets and boxes enhance a bathroom's decorative ambience while housing larger supplies. A large basket set in a corner of the bathroom floor provides a repository for extra toilet tissue. Bath towels can be easily replaced when a fresh set is stored in an open receptacle within fingertips' reach.

Baskets and boxes can themselves be stored within a deep cabinet, but a more prac-

tical solution for organizing hidden supplies is using stackable plastic tubs. Cleaning rags find a ready home here, with cleaning products stacked neatly on top in a tub of their own. Remember to apply the same organizational principles to your interior storage spaces as to your exterior ones to ensure optimum efficiency and success for your space.

Long, vertical organizers that attach to the showerhead provide space for shampoos and soaps. Other bath caddies come in tray form,

This lovely vignette demonstrates a charming way to present amenities to guests. A bowl of soap atop a picnic basket that serves as a hamper and a tiny stool piled with towels creates a sense of welcome.

spanning horizontally across the width of the tub. These can pushed to the rear of the tub when a shower is desired, or moved to the middle during a bath. They work especially well for storing kids' bath toys.

Storage carts work very well in bathrooms. Mounted on casters, these can be pushed to a corner of the room when not in use. Plastic-coated wire cages with pullout metal bins that stack like gymnasium lockers are also appropriate for some bathrooms. With their no-nonsense look, they're ideal for lofts or high-tech designs in which exposed ductwork and structural members are an integral part of the design. The cage (which includes a metal frame for housing the individual bins) can substitute for cabinetry in a bathroom that lacks linen storage areas, with towels and rags, as well as toiletries and boxes of tissues conveniently stored in the stacked bins.

Optimizing Your Bathroom Shelves

Bathroom shelves should conform to the contents being stored on them. In most new homes, shelves in linen closets and cabinets are usually too deep and span too much vertical space to be functional for storage. This is especially true for towel shelves—it's no fun

reaching for your towel of choice from the bottom of a stack when the stack is more than a few towels high.

Short of building new cabinets with shelves at more compatible heights, it's possible to make your storage more functional and efficient by altering the placement of your existing shelving. Remount shelves at closer intervals and you'll create shallower spaces for stacking of bath linens. You can also employ shelf dividers that will allow you to make better use of your deep storage, or recruit deep tubs or baskets to store infrequently used items

Recruited from the kitchen, this baker's rack provides a wonderful service in this bathroom. Its shelves are perfect for holding towels or plants and flowers that brighten the space. The curlicue design of the wrought iron piece fits right into the countrified decor.

in the back of cabinets on shelves. Store your towels or toiletries used daily toward the front.

When two shelves are placed too close together to allow you to store the items you deem appropriate for that space, subtract a shelf. Simply removing a single shelf can open up the cabinet space to house the taller goods you need to store there.

A Bathtub Frame

Hot-tub manufacturers made this solution mainstream by creating frames around their product to enhance function and appearance. But the same can be done to an ordinary home bathtub. Given enough room (about a foot [30.5cm] at the side of the tub or at one or both of its ends), extending the tub with a

Building shelves within easy reach of your bathtub, as this laminate example demonstrates, optimizes your bathing time and experience since it keeps all that you need close to you. It also sets the stage for a display that promotes a sense of tranquility.

wooden frame is an affordable, inventive way to increase storage capacity.

When the tub is built in to the walls at both ends, as most are in newer houses, a side frame on the tub's long, open side will be the best storage solution. Build platforms aligned with the tub's top and bottom. That will create a recessed space for storing everything from towels to toiletries. Add sliding or pullout doors for enclosed storage. If the tub isn't built in to the wall at the ends, you can build a storage headboard and footboard. At the head of the tub, the frame can even be built up taller than the tub height, with shelf space in the middle. The lower part can be shorter and enclosed, used to store towels or bath products.

A Toilet Wall

The areas to either side of the toilet are typically dead space, perhaps storing only a bottle of toilet bowl cleaner and a brush, and maybe a plunger. But with a little imagination, these areas can become functional, good-looking storage spaces.

When building a shelving unit around the toilet, extend it to the ceiling and make the

OPPOSITE AND ABOVE: The bathtub frames on these two pages were made from tile for water resistance and give the rooms a clean look. The frame on the left extends at the foot and provides a great built-in receptacle for towels. Above, the frame creates a platform for stepping into the tub, as well as display areas for flowers and more. Towels are stored right over the foot of the tub for optimum convenience. A painted white corner cabinet holds soaps and bath oils.

Use rough, forgiving redwood or cedar and leave nail heads exposed for a rustic feel. If you don't want to build your own frame, you can purchase one to fit your bath at any home store.

Wall-Mounted Shelves

New cabinetry is expensive, especially when its addition requires structural changes. A far less expensive option to improving bathroom storage is wall-mounted shelves. Antique shelves in their original paint can enhance the ambience of a country decor; glass shelves will continue the sleek look desired in a contemporary bathroom.

shelf depth the same as that of the toilet tank's extrusion into the room. Shelves should be built against the sides of the tank to ensure a built-in look. Be sure not to build shelves directly on top of the tank—leave enough room for easy removal of the tank lid when there are plumbing problems. You don't need to be a master carpenter to create a toilet frame.

ABOVE LEFT: In this bath, a double-doored cabinet and single shelf were added in what may have otherwise been wasted space. A black lacquer box atop a table on the left provides storage for toiletries and creates a wonderful decorative accent. ABOVE RIGHT: A couple shelves were added to accommodate an overflow of toiletries in this bath and provide a spot on which to rest the sink's overhead mirror. OPPOSITE: A glass-fronted wall-mounted cabinet was added to give this sparse bathroom style. Robes are suspended from hooks on the wall behind the generously sized tub for easy access.

Ready-Made Cabinetry

New cabinets can be added to increase bathroom storage without incurring expense and time and without the stress of living in a construction zone. Wall-hung, ready-made cabinets and prefabricated bathroom vanities are quick, easy storage solutions. One or two wall-mounted cabinets may be all you need. Be sure to locate these cabinets in a place

A wall currently dominated by a towel rack also has room to install a shelf or two above. Also, the area behind the toilet is often dead space and is an ideal spot to locate a couple of tiered shelves or a manufactured curio shelving unit (wicker and rattan shelf units are available for little expense at import shops, discount stores, and craft stores).

Corner shelves that span the entire height of a room don't take up any essential wall space but offer a place for housing odds and ends such as magazines and paperbacks or a fresh bouquet of flowers in a bud vase.

ABOVE LEFT: A glass shelf between his-and-her sinks in this bath allows space for a picture frame and accessories and connects the two grooming areas. A thin towel bar beneath holds hand towels for guests. ABOVE RIGHT: Most sinks today are designed with an enclosed vanity to store bathroom essentials. These can easily be built around the plumbing hardware of an existing sink for added storage possibilities, as is the case in this bathroom. A medicine cabinet above stores smaller items, such as toothbrushes, toothpaste, and medication.

where their projection into the room won't entail bumping heads or creating cramped quarters (for example, you don't want to hang a cabinet on a wall where you typically stand to dry off from the bath). The wall space above the toilet is an ideal spot for hanging a cabinet.

A ready-made vanity is an affordable option to having one custom-made. These vanities come in all price ranges, depending upon the style and quality of materials they are fabricated from, so make sure you research your options and preferences thoroughly before making a purchase. Most importantly, always know your bathroom's dimensions when you shop.

Skirted Answers

When adding extra architecture to your bathroom isn't desired, your storage solution may be as simple as adding a fabric skirt to your sink. Skirting your sink or toilet with a floor-length print or another fabric that is compatible with the room's decor adds a flirty charm to the space while creating a hidden storage niche for any number of bathroom items.

Creating a skirt is an easy task that you need only rudimentary sewing skills to complete. Stitch an elastic band at the top of the fabrics you've chosen to adhere to the sink or

At first it seems that this vanity is really a chest of drawers brought in from another room in the home, but look again: a sink is built into the top. The drawers store everything from towels to spillover clothes from the bedroom. The medicine cabinet door slides open, instead of opening out into the room, allowing the owner to still have access to the mirror while he fishes around for a toothbrush or shaving cream.

Creating a Closet

toilet top, then hem the bottom at the point where it touches the floor or allow it to puddle on the floor. Puddled skirts add a more voluptuous, soft look to the space that's especially nice when a romantic or whimsical mood is desired. Items that may otherwise be eyesores can be stored away in plastic stackable tubs or pullout stackable wire shelving units and kept discreetly out of view beneath the floor-length fabric.

If you have a lot of extra space in your bathroom, you may consider adding a closet. Because it is custom-created to your needs, this storage closet can employ every free inch of space, from ceiling to floor, to address storage. Louvered or solid-wood sliding or bifold doors create a sleek, streamlined effect that's a bonus for bathroom designs that require a clean and simple look.

Another alternative to building an enclosed cabinet is to skirt your sink. Here, the plaid fabric chosen is in the same palette as the bathroom, but contrasts with the otherwise feminine details of the space.

A half closet was built into a spare wall adjacent to the toilet to accommodate guest towels, extra soap, and all amenities for an efficient bathroom installation.

CHAPTER FIVE

The Bedroom

Of all the rooms in the home, it is vital that the bedroom have an uncluttered feel. After all, bedrooms are the private sanctuaries of those who inhabit them. Translated into criteria for storage, this means that the bedroom must somehow accommodate clothing and personal items without intruding too obviously into the visual landscape of the space. Achieving this is considerable, given a bedroom's typical limited area and the number of items to be contained therein.

In addition to providing the most efficient storage possible, the bedroom also has to reflect the occupants' personalities. This means arriving at a fine balance between the concealment and display of objects. Not all clothing and accessories must be stashed behind closed doors or in drawers. Decorative items—a collection of ethnic jewelry, colorful ties, or interesting handbags—can be stored within plain view, given the proper organization and presentation.

Take the time to thoroughly analyze every bit of existing space in your bedroom for storage possibilities, from walls and floors to furnishings and closets.

This carefully planned bedroom is the perfect retreat from the chaos of the outside world. Its simple design and spare ornamentation exude the feel of an uncluttered lifestyle. Belongings are cleverly stowed away in enormous closets that flank a minimalist fireplace.

The Bedroom Closet

Without a doubt, the greatest storage opportunities in the bedroom are in the closet. Anything can be stored here, regardless of appearance. Thanks to manufacturers' responses to consumers' needs for more efficient closets, a number of organizers are now available to address every storage requirement.

The typical bedroom closet requires a little ingenuity to make it a functional storage receptacle for the bedroom's myriad needs. It usually includes only a rod mounted high on the walls for long garments such as dresses and coats. While not sufficient in itself, the high rod is necessary to provide wrinkle-free space for dresses and trousers hung full-length rather than folded.

Additionally, the well-designed bedroom closet should include space for hanging shorter wearables: shirts, blouses, skirts, pants, and suits. For maximum efficiency, mount two rods, one above the other. Having this tiered pair of rods ensures optimum use of vertical space.

A third requirement for the efficient closet is storage for stackable clothing—an area devoted to drawers, shallow shelves, or portable stacked bins or boxes to hold folded garments and permit easy retrieval.

A final area of storage provided by the ideal bedroom closet is a space for shoes. This space is one of the easiest to graft onto the closet, as any number of shoe organizers are suitable, from hanging organizers that fit on back of the closet door to freestanding systems that occupy the floor. An upper shelf space for stashing odds and ends such as briefcases, beach bags, small luggage, hat boxes, and other items not in constant use is also desirable.

A storage-efficient walk-in closet is a dream come true. Here, there is a place for everything. To the left, two tiers of clothes are hung. The back section is divided to house a collection of hats. Closed-off drawers below hold lingerie, socks, and other small garments. On the right, cabinets contain important papers. Shoes find a comfortable home below on slanted shelves for easy access.

Configuring Your Closet

Mount rods about sixty-nine inches (175cm) from the floor for long garments. For a pair of stacked rods for shorter separates, mount the upper rod seventy-six to eighty-four inches (193 to 213cm) above the floor, the lower rod thirty-six to forty-two inches (91.5 to 107cm) above the floor. To ensure enough width for your clothing to hang wrinkle-free, position rods twelve to fourteen inches (30.5 to 35.5cm) from the back wall. For other apparel, allocate about eight inches (20cm) for every ten garments, reserving more space for bulkier coats and suits.

Above the upper rod, mount a shelf for hat boxes and other infrequently used items. In the center of the closet on the back wall between the two ends of rod systems, create a storage area of your choice for stacked clothing, using either a store-bought modular closet organizer or a wall of shelves you build yourself.

When choosing a modular system, select a variety with components having dimensions that, when assembled in the configuration that best meets your needs, make maximum use of wall space without intruding into the hanging-garments area. Leave space at the floor for a freestanding shoe rack, or divide your wall-mounted shelves into smaller com-

partments that are each sized to hold a pair of shoes. If you need all of the center wall space to store folded garments, hang a shoe caddy on the back of the door.

OPPOSITE: This closet was designed with every apparel consideration in mind, right down to the hook on the door that holds a robe. The top shelf stores an extra blanket for chilly nights. Rows of shoes are separated by a shelf for hosiery and a hatbox. Compartments of various sizes were designed for different styles of handbags. Directly below, blouses and short dresses find a home. Pull-out drawers accommodate everything from jewelry to lingerie. ABOVE: Ample closet space and a built-in "chest of drawers" in this cleanly designed bedroom conceal clothes and accessories behind closed doors.

Determining your needs will dictate which system works best for you. Instead of mounting the long-garment rack at the same level as the upper short-garment rod, position it a foot (30.5cm) or more lower, allowing clothing to hang without touching the floor but freeing up space above the rod for a small shelf for plastic stackable boxes stocked with T-shirts,

Having separate compartments for pairs of shoes keeps them not only well-organized but looking good. Two dowels for hanging clothes and shelves are all that are needed to accommodate apparel in this closet.

lingerie, and other small garments. Or work out another configuration that frees up more shelf space above a rod for a neat presentation of shoes. Consider dividing the closet's top shelf into compartments just wide and tall enough for efficient storage of boots. When hanging and stackable clothing is stored efficiently at either end of the closet, the center back wall can be put to another use. Pegboard or a lattice-style pegged rack can be added for hats, necklaces, purses, ties, headbands, and other accessories.

His-and-her closets are separated by a narrow chest of drawers topped by a whimsical hat on a stand. In each closet, shoes are kept separated to help maintain their good condition. "His" closet also features an additional set of drawers.

To determine the effectiveness of your closet solution, look at your hanging garments. Are all of the longer ones grouped together on one or more high-mounted rods? Are all of the shorter garments hanging from rods that use only enough vertical space to accommodate them? Are folding clothes organized in drawers, shelves, or portable containers that are accessible, in shallow stacks that won't topple? Are shoes arranged so that all can be seen, with none hidden behind the hems of long-hanging apparel or in back recesses that require digging to find?

ABOVE: Accessories such as belts and ties can make a decorative statement of their own hanging in an orderly fashion on an available portion of the wall. This method also provides unbelievably easy access to these items. BELOW: Trunks have always made great receptacles for bedroom storage. Here, a trunk in a wood that matches the glorious four-poster bed is a great place to stash anything from extra blankets to sweaters.

Once you've established that items are properly organized, make sure you haven't missed any potential storage space. On the walls devoted to rods, is the full length from floor to ceiling being used? The floor should provide some storage function beneath hanging apparel, as the area above the top rack should be enlisted as shelf space. Is there a blank wall anywhere? If so, consider hanging pegboard, special wall-mounted tie or belt organizers, a series of individual hooks, or additional shelving.

Furniture Options

One of the best ways to conquer storage problems in your bedroom is to get smart with furnishings. Each piece in the room should address storage as part of its function.

Beds

Beds that include storage case goods, headboards, and footboards have been around for decades. If your storage needs are great, it only makes sense to put the dead space behind the head of the bed and at its foot to work.

This platform bed is cleverly configured with shelving on one side to hold books and other reading materials. The headboard also opens to provide more much-needed storage of spare blankets and the like.

The biggest potential drawback in selecting such a bed is that its style, which is often utilitarian in design, may be incompatible with the style of your room. But you can use your imagination and alter the look of the bed with decorative paintwork. Even a secondhand bed in a bland, dark wood can be transformed into a flight of fancy with an easy-to-apply floral stenciling design. The bolder artist can experiment with freehand designs for a one-of-a-kind effect. With no more expense than that of a can of paint, your bed can become the pièce de résistance of your room, customized in a way no factory bed could ever be.

Who says a storage-savvy furnishing can't have a wonderful design as well? This bed is the centerpiece of this room and is chock full of storage potential, including a chest of drawers at the headboard, small closets at either end, drawers at the base, and a bookshelf inside. Because the bed doesn't go all the way to the ceiling, colorful boxes can be stored on top, adding an additional decorative touch.

You can create a similar storage system with your existing bed. Pull the bed about one foot (30.5cm) out from the wall at its head and build a shelving unit that wraps around the bed. The unit can be as long as the area just above the back of the bed, or it can extend to either side to create built-in nightstands. Or, if there is no door or window on the same wall as the bed, do-it-yourself shelving can span the entire wall in width and height. This shelving wall creates a wonderful streamlined look and eliminates the need for small, space-eating furnishings that eat up both horizontal and vertical space.

Floor space at the foot of the bed has long been recognized for its storage potential. Many a grandmother's house featured a cedar chest or trunk here where keepsakes or quilts were kept. A chest or a low table or bench for surface storage can be added here.

Pull-out drawers were added below this Nantucket bed in an attic bedroom because adding a separate chest of drawers would eat up precious space that is already at a minimum due to the slanted ceilings.

Storage potential is most prominent beneath the bed. Some beds are designed with wide, deep pullout drawers in the space beneath the mattress. You can create similar storage in this area without much difficulty. Large drawers from an inexpensive secondhand dresser or chest can be fitted with casters and rolled out of view when not in use. Less frequently used garments such as accessories or seasonal items can be easily stored in portable organizers—covered cardboard boxes, cedar boxes or drawers, zip-up stackable bags, wire bins or drawers, or clear plastic boxes.

ABOVE: Privacy and high function all in one, this bed is almost completely enclosed in a wooden storage unit that also serves as a wardrobe and a chest of drawers. BELOW: The Murphy bed certainly presents a great alternative when opting for an uncluttered decor. When not in use, the bed is pushed up and enclosed in a cabinet system that also includes closet space.

Armoires

An absence of closets in a bedroom doesn't necessarily mean forgoing storage in that room. Vintage or modern armoires can either substitute for a closet altogether or augment the limited storage capacity of a small closet while imbuing the bedroom with warmth and charm.

Today's armoires are designed to store not only hanging clothes and folded garments but home electronics equipment as well. Most are available with a vacant inner cabinet that can be customized to meet the owner's needs, with shelf, drawer, cabinet, and rod placement left to the owner's specifications. When a TV, VCR, and stereo need to be stored away, spaces can be outfitted in the armoire's interior. The electronics equipment can be concealed behind the armoire's doors when not in use. If home entertainment equipment has been deemed for storage in another receptacle in the room, the entire armoire can be customized for clothing storage.

When seeking a storage piece for clothing, consider the armoire's capacity to house both hanging and folded clothing. If only folded-garment storage is required, a dresser or chest of drawers may be adequate for your needs. The armoire's height makes better use of vertical wall space than dressers or most chests, making it the most efficient selection when all other deciding factors are equal.

In lieu of an industrial-looking home-entertainment center, a decorative armoire will perform the same function without compromising traditional style. And, when not in use, your electronic equipment can be concealed behind beautifully painted wood doors.

Home Entertainment Centers

Like those designed for the public rooms of the home, bedroom-scaled wall units are offered in virtually any design style imaginable, from contemporary or country to traditional or more whimsical eclectic.

Designed especially to house electronics, the home entertainment center provides storage space for CDs, tapes, and videos. Additionally, it can display collectibles, books, and functional items such as a clock and telephone. The personal computer can also can be incorporated into its storage, with a shelf configuration geared toward a home office.

One of the drawbacks of this furnishing is that it occupies a significant amount of available wall space. When only one wall of the room is without windows or doors, it may not be practical to devote it to a furnishing that

OPPOSITE: A shortage of available closets did not prevent the inhabitants of this space from having an uncluttered life. An armoire was commissioned and outfitted with various shelves and hardware for storing all kinds of garments. ABOVE: Conventional storage alternatives were employed to create clutter-free decor in this bedroom. A wicker chest of drawers holds clothing while an armoire painted in muted earth tones conceals a home-entertainment center.

can't be used to store clothing and accessories. When wall space is available, however, the piece offers the advantage of being mobile: unlike built-in shelving, it can be moved to a new location to provide storage when it's needed in another room.

Fitted for clothing as well as for a TV, this armoire can tuck both away when the TV is not in use. Two compartments above the TV are the perfect size for a VCR and CD player.

Crates and Boxes

Instead of utilizing floor space beside a reading chair with a storage-poor lamp stand or small side table, substitute boxes or old shipping crates. These can provide a hiding place for infrequently used items while still serving as a table surface. The more unexpected the solution, the more the space is enhanced with character. Seek options that are fun to provide the room with personality.

Built-In Options

When walls are dominated by furnishings that don't make optimum use of floor-to-ceiling space, adding shelves can be a good solution. Span an entire wall or even the entire room with one contiguous shelf. Shelving painted to match the room's architectural wood trim weaves the space together while making each wall available for storage.

For the collector, this addition provides a

ABOVE LEFT: Opt for a night table with high storage potential—here you can store everything from treasured mementos to books to remote control devices for the TV and the stereo. ABOVE RIGHT: Opting for built-in storage is wise in the bedroom as well as any other room in the home. Here, custom-designed shelving conforms to the curve of the walls.

while providing space for perfumes or cosmetics. You can customize cabinets with a coat of paint or a decorative paint treatment. Painting cabinets to coordinate with a painted wooden chair or chest creates a pulled-together look.

A sunny bedroom window ideal for an easy chair or chaise lounge may also be a great location for a window seat. This architectural add-on is easily constructed by building a simple wooden box out from the wall to the

display area for a wealth of objects. (A key principle in providing organized storage with a clean look is grouping like objects en masse rather than scattering them throughout a space.) Functional items can be planted here, offering an unexpected visual delight: a wall lined with a woman's colorful pumps liberates closet space for other storage purposes and provides immediate access.

Instead of shelving, try hanging suspended cabinets. A pair of cabinets suspended on either side of a dresser mirror creates a symmetrical balance that's aesthetically pleasing

ABOVE LEFT: Avid readers enjoy a dream bedroom, replete with a two-level overhead book shelving system and night stands that are designed to hold books. ABOVE RIGHT: Storage was certainly considered in an extra bedroom used by a toy collector. Here, an over-the-bed shelf holds antique toys and nostalgic advertisements that serve to decorate the room.

floor, under the windowsill. Top the seating area with soft cushions and throw pillows in fabrics that contribute to the room's overall decorating scheme.

One of the simplest ways of creating storage in the window seat is to build a lift-up seat, which allows items to be tucked discreetly out of sight. Another option is to construct the window seat so that the front opens with sliding or pull-open doors. The latter construction method is recommended to store more frequently used items.

The symmetry of the two window seats flanking this vanity table and mirror lends added elegance to this boudoir. The cushions atop the seats have been upholstered in a fabric that echos the carpet's floral border, blending the seats into the room's decor.

Children's Bedrooms

Kids' rooms need storage solutions all their own. Unless properly addressed, storage of a child's toys, books, and clothing can become a parent's nightmare.

Let go of the idea that all of your child's belongings need to be stored behind closed doors. Employing both closed and open storage will result in organizing a plethora of goods and adding character.

Organize the closet the same way you would an adult's closet: allocate shelves, drawers, and portable containers for clothes and toys. When

A little girl's room can be a wonderful play station as well as a beautifully decorated space. Shelving built around a large window accommodates some of her favorite things. The window ledge created by the shelving unit also provides a place to keep pictures and keepsakes.

Large colorful bins in primary colors placed on the floor are much more conducive to a child putting his or her toys away than in a closet that requires sliding or pulling open doors or drawers. Hanging fishnet baskets are another creative solution for openly storing play items.

A natural tendency for kids is to "clean" by pushing items under the bed. Outfit the beneath-the-bed space with drawers on casters. This will help the child develop organizational skills. The room can be cleaned in seconds flat—but in a systematic way.

space in the room is restricted, consider putting one of the child's play units—a tea table or a desk—in the center of the closet. This can prove a fun hideout for the child. Make sure the closet is well lit and ventilated and that the door is not prone to getting stuck.

Within the room itself, make sure every space is working to satisfy storage needs. A single row of easy-to-add shelving along the perimeter of the walls within the child's reach makes a great storehouse for stuffed animals. Devoting a smaller wall to a freestanding furnishing with shelves provides additional storage space for a tidy display of playthings.

ABOVE LEFT: Two pyramidal bookcases store all the accouterments of childhood while giving this upscale children's bedroom a touch of style. The vanity has been skirted to conceal stored toys. As this is a child's room, the fireplace is not functional and provides yet another nook in which to stow stuff away. ABOVE RIGHT: This Victorian white iron child's bed is sided by a cabinet and ample chest of drawers. The dollhouse is actually not a dollhouse at all but an armoire to hold surplus clothing.

Finding storage-wise furnishings is easy for a child's room. Manufacturers offer furniture wall systems that are storage-savvy, with capacious drawers and cabinets that utilize every available inch. Even children's beds are constructed with storage efficiency in mind, some offering play towers as part of an upper bunk for stashing toys and stuffed animals. By taking the time to find the right furniture, you can provide an orderly environment for the child who has everything, even in a small room.

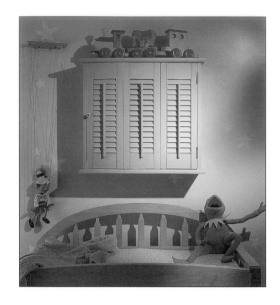

ABOVE: A baby blue cupboard over a changing table is the perfect place to keep lotions, powders, ointments, and wipes for baby. The shutterlike appearance of the doors make the unit appear to be a window that opens out to a night sky. BELOW: A window seat that spans nearly the entire wall makes for the perfect toy chest in this child's attic bedroom. The skirted table hides favorite toys and keeps them readily accessible to the child.

A bookshelf with a crenellated top situated between two beds serves the dual purpose of storage receptacle and room divider in this room shared by a couple of brothers.

CHAPTER SIX

Other Storage Possibilities

When the storage capacity of the major rooms of the home is filled, even the most inventive solutions for where to put things won't be adequate. Thankfully, most houses are blessed with extra spaces that can accommodate over-flow—areas in the home where odds and ends from Christmas decorations to old Boy Scout uniforms can be kept. As these areas are often unseen by guests, they are sometimes over-cluttered embarrassments. Given the right storage solutions, these spaces can become efficiently designed and presentable.

Attics and Basements

These mostly unfinished spaces are usually hidden from guests' view and as a result end up being "junk rooms" in most homes. These areas usually invite the unattractive accumula-tion of shipping boxes and items that should be sold at a garage sale or given away. But when the proper storage solutions are employed, these rooms will look better.

Seasonal decorations don't have to be stored away in boxes when not in use. Your attic or basement can become a year-long showroom for your favorite and most fragile ornaments and bibelots, as well as for strands of Christmas lights. Because these rooms aren't in regular view, they don't have to con-form to the style of the rest of the home—you have creative license here. Hammer nails into walls and create Christmas tree outlines with the nails. Then string the lights over the nails to create "Christmas trees" that you can then hang individual ornaments on. Strands of lights can also be mounted across the perime-ter of the room or in more creative swags or patterns to prevent breakage and knots.

Sports equipment can also be stored in a similar fashion. While some of these pieces will probably be included in the main rooms of the home, this solution offers the opportu-nity to store beloved out-of-season sporting goods in view. Keep all related items together and mount them on the wall to create unusu-al art objects out of golf clubs, bike helmets, horse bridles and halters, and tennis rackets. Display trophies on wall-mounted shelves nearby. Devote more wall space to framed sports-related photographs, posters, or

The attic is among the best places to store things because of its isolated location. And trunks make perfect receptacles for a wealth of items from old clothes to schoolwork from years past. In this attic, trunks are neatly lined up against the wall, allowing ample room to walk through. A chest of drawers and a table at the far end of the space store more delicate items.

ribbons, especially important ones from your childhood that you can't part with. Even sports-related accessories will find a happy home stored this way.

Paperback books can be easily stored here. Books can get moldy when packed away in boxes—a better solution is to create a paperback library to give these books a rightful place on shelves. By mounting a few shelves directly onto the top half of a wall, a library look can be achieved without sacrificing wall space for other storage needs.

Because the wise collector knows the value of rotation—not displaying all collectibles at one time—the junk room can become a gallery of sorts. Collectibles out of circulation in public rooms can be presented in all their glory on furniture, shelves, or even work tables. This method of storage is preferable to boxes, as it makes retrieval much more immediate.

Special Closets

Each closet in the home has the potential, regardless of its size, to be reshaped with closet organizers to meet your storage needs. The types of organizers you use will depend upon the nature of the objects to be stored.

For greatest efficiency, try to focus on objects that will be used within the proximity of that closet. There may be no need for hanging rods in nonbedroom closets. A floor-to-ceiling shelving configuration may be the best solution here. For example, instead of cramming all of your sheet music into your piano bench, organize it neatly in folders or boxes and stack those in the closet.

ABOVE: Placing a cabinet at the end of a hallway will provide storage for everything from extra pillows to toiletries, as demonstrated here. OPPOSITE: An overflow of books from a home's vast library finds a home in this traditionally styled armoire. A collection of figurines occupies the top two shelves.

You may consider creating a display area in your closet. Instead of fitting your closet with predominately practical organizers, install pegboard displays (for hanging vintage beaded bags, for example) and wood or glass shelves. You may even want to remove the closet door to allow continual viewing. Be sure to consider lighting when choosing this option. Small spots shining down or up on art objects creates a dramatic effect. For the beachcomber or rock-collecting hiker who enjoys reminders of favorite outdoor moments but doesn't have adequate display space in rooms, a closet display area may be the perfect answer to easily preserving memories and keeping your home uncluttered at the same time.

Building a wooden cabinet onto a wall will create a place to keep a variety of items not frequently used, such as these different-sized baskets, which are storage receptacles in themselves, safe and dust-free.

Garages

Garages store more than vehicles. Special wall-mounted organizers for garden and household tools are available at any hardware store and will work wonders in your garage. Mounted vertically, these devices conserve horizontal shelf space; mounted horizontally, with tools laid on their sides, the organizers occupy little vertical space, allowing for several different types of organizers to be stacked on top of each other. Whatever the configuration, these will make access to the tools incredibly easy.

For sharp tools such as axes, saws, and spades that could endanger persons stumbling over them or prove a real threat to curious kids, the wall-mounted solution is a perfect safety solution. Make certain the most potentially harmful tools are stored high on the wall, well out of a child's reach or an adult's accidental brush.

Products associated with the lawn, garden, household maintenance, or construction will find a logical home in the garage. Nails make perfect hangers for garden fencing, wire tomato cages, various hoses, and paintbrushes. Lawn

When organized properly, your garage can satisfy many different storage requirements. Here, hooks were installed on the walls to keep garden tools and brooms out of the way. A set of wire compartments holds tools, screws, nails, and small cans of paint, and also serves as a workstation. Bags of pet food, potting soil, and other odds and ends are suspended from the door on smaller wire racks.

mowers, weed cutters, and snowblowers guzzle up a lot of garage space, especially when cars are parked in the garage. Group these together in one area that offers partial shelter—perhaps beneath a workbench. Or build a small closet on one wall. The convenience it will provide will be well worth the effort and minimal expense. (A closet designed for a garage can be makeshift, using secondhand or rudimentary doors—or maybe no door at all.)

For any homeowner with power tools, a work bench is another addition that's affordable, easy to add, and extremely beneficial in freeing up other space. The work bench has the added bonus of protecting both the tools and people—especially small children, who might be tempted to play with the tools if they are within easy reach. The wall behind the work bench is the ideal location for storing smaller items associated with power tools or with building projects in general, offering optimum efficiency by saving time and steps when working on a project at the bench.

By outfitting one end of the garage with shelves, cabinets, or a freestanding cupboard when space permits, the passionate gardener can obtain all the potting-shed storage he or she needs. Lining an old secondhand drawer with aluminum foil provides space for storing potting soil or fertilizers. Terra-cotta pots of all

This garage is also a home office and library. Books are neatly stored on laminate shelves mounted around a window on the far wall. The space that is left between the top shelf and the peaked ceiling provides a wonderful display opportunity for collected pieces.

shapes and sizes become an art statement when presented en masse along a garage wall's shelf or shelves.

Bicycles don't need to impede the garage's traffic flow. They can be stored within plain sight and easy access on the walls. Use plastic-coated hooks available at any hardware store. Be sure to hang the bikes from their frames, not their wheels—wheels lose their shape when suspended from their rims and you may also damage the spokes. Also store bike helmets directly on the wall. Any other sports equipment not already stored within the home can be stored on garage walls—tennis rackets, skis, float tubes, even a canoe.

Because smooth, unimpeded pedestrian traffic flow is an essential consideration, garage benches are a storage option many homeowners appreciate. Lined against the walls, they can accommodate storage along their surface and underneath. Be sure your garage's traffic lanes won't be restricted by the ten inches (25.5cm) or so of walking space benches will eat with their width.

By mounting bicycles on a wall in your garage, you alleviate the risk of tripping over them and you also keep them safe and in good working order—tires won't deplete as easily and the bicycles will be off the floor where moisture might gather and cause rust and corrosion.

Laundry Rooms

The laundry room is an ideal place to store a number of items. Plastic-coated wall-mounted shelves in different depths and lengths provide a convenient location for storing laundry detergents, bleaches, and fabric softener, but clothing and linens freshly folded from the dryer can also be implemented here when there isn't enough time after folding to put these in their proper places.

A utility cart on casters that can be rolled out of the way when not in use is another storage option that's handy here. Lay wet laundry as it comes out of the washing machine here, allowing all the clothes to be removed at one time and then loaded into the dryer. The cart can be used to hold folded laundry as well.

By hanging rods near the dryer, you can avoid wrinkling hanging garments that have just been laundered. Dresses and trousers can be placed on coat hangers and hung on the rod until it's time to move them to their closets.

Small laundry rooms may not have adequate space for an ironing board. This storage problem can easily be solved by adding a wall-mounted version that attaches to the back of the door. The laundry room may also be a good space to store small stools and stepladders. When folded, you can adhere a stepladder directly to the wall with nails or hooks. The stool can serve as a place to sit while folding laundry.

The laundry room is also a good site for storing sewing-related equipment. Spools of colorful thread and reams of yarn for knitting or crocheting can be displayed on shelves along the laundry room walls to create a cheerful ambience and solve a vital storage need. Sewing baskets and fabrics can also be stored this way. Putting threads and needles in the laundry room also makes functional sense: when garments lose buttons in the dryer, these can be sewn on immediately before they get lost.

ABOVE: This laundry room has been perfectly configured to have a spare look. The ironing board collapses and folds up into the closet behind it. Two rows of enclosed cabinetry hold detergents and other laundry essentials, as well as a supply of hangers. The unit to the left is compartmentalized to help sort laundry by family member and the top surface of the unit serves as a folding station. OPPOSITE: Cleverly and conveniently positioned between kitchen and living room, this laundry room literally disappears when not in use. The ironing board, washing machine, and dryer can all be concealed behind closed doors.

Guest Bedrooms

Few homes have enough space to spare to reserve a guest bedroom just for housing overnight guests. The room must somehow address the day-to-day lifestyle needs of the owners—especially their storage problems.

Keep an upper and lower drawer free of garments for guests, then use the rest of a chest of drawers free for your out-of-season storage. Similarly, hang off-season clothes in this closet, leaving room for guests to hang garments.

Do you have extra throw pillows for your sofa, but nowhere to store them? Plan the guest room's color scheme to fit the pillows' palette and keep these pillows on the guest room bed. Do you have a montage of sixties memorabilia that you don't want to throw away but have no room for? Theme the guest room in that era and solve your storage issue while also providing a fun environment for your overnight visitors.

Given the right antique or whimsical furnishings, a guest room can also be a place for storing old stuffed animals and toys. Provide wall shelves just as you would in a child's room for displaying these memories in proud

ABOVE RIGHT: A chest of many-sized drawers presents a storehouse of solutions for stowing everything from small garments and personal items to collectibles. It also makes a wonderful decorative statement. ABOVE LEFT: A guest room is a great place to put extra, off-season clothes and items not used every day. Here, the closet doors have been decorated with cut-out felt snakes to enhance the room's Southwestern theme.

view. Kids' artwork can also pile up in boxes and drawers. Why not take the best, frame it or dry-mount it, then hang it as artwork in the guest room?

Storage needs associated with hobbies such as sewing or crafts or with a home office can be efficiently addressed in the guest room. Planned wisely, even a pint-size bedroom can be furnished with a bed and some clothing storage features while having room to spare for a small computer desk, sewing machine, or crafts table. By making the room multipurpose, you haven't detracted from its primary role—you'll simply give that role deeper dimension. Just as you would select furniture to solve storage problems in a small bedroom, choose furniture for this room that will house office supplies or hobby-related equipment.

An armoire was added to this tranquil country-style guest bedroom to store clothing as well as conceal a TV. A small trunk at the foot of the bed is a special place to store small items. Baskets and boxes from the household find a home on top of the armoire and enhance the charming decor. They are also storage receptacles in themselves.

Sources

pages 2, 46
Jim Sterling
Portland, ME
(207) 772-0037

pages 3,5,10
Jane Langmuir
Providence, RI
(401) 331-3039

pages 7, 43, 83
Chris Barrett
8811 Alden Ave. Suite 6
Los Angeles, CA 90048

page 9, 104 left
Anne Lenox
Partners in Design
Newton, MA
(617) 244-3360

page 12
Centerbrook Architects
Centerbrook, CT
(860) 767-0175

pages 13, 33 right
Kitchens by Deane
1267 E. Main St.
Stanford, CT 06902

pages 19, 30
Frank Israel
254 S. Robertson Blvd.
Los Angeles, CA 90211

page 21
Gayle Reynolds
ASID
Lexington, MA
(617) 861-9712

pages 25, 32, 39
John Martin
Torrington, CT
(860) 496-1233

Bullock and Company
Creemore, Ontario
(705) 466-2505

page 29
Warner Cunningham Architects
Brookline, MA
(617) 566-1644

pages 34, 38, 49 right, 66 right, 79, 88
Carole Kaplan
Two By Two Interior Design
Andover, MA
(508) 470-3131

page 36
Annie Kelly
2074 Watsonia Terrace
Los Angeles, CA 90068

page 41
Daly-Genik
Los Angeles, CA
(310) 656-3180

page 42
P.J. Wheeler Association
Boston, MA

pages 50, 55, 63, 67, 86-87
John Scholz
Camden, ME
(207) 236-0777

page 51
Judy Kenyon
1755 Warwick Rd.
San Marino, CA 91108

page 52
Dan McGilvrey/Roger Schaw
TGAR Architecture
165 8 St.
San Francisco, CA 94103

page 53 right
Beverly Payeff
Brookline, NH

page 53 left
Marshall Lewis
721 Latimer Rd
Santa Monica, CA 90402

page 54 right
Ericson Antique Stoves
Littleton, MA

page 56 top
Berg Howland Association
Cambridge, MA
(617) 661-2030

pages 64, 81
Joe Ruggiero
4512 Louise Ave.
Encino, CA 91316

page 65 left
Theodore & Theodore

pages 65 right, 66 left
Killory

page 77
Kitchens by Krengel
1688 Grand Ave.
St. Paul, MN 55105

page 84
Susan Armstrong Interior Design
Concord, MA
(508) 369-8444

pages 90, 94 top
Maxine Ordesky
240 S. Linden Dr.
Beverly Hills, CA 90212

page 94 bottom
Kelsey Maddox-Bell
P.P. Box 741
Kilaeua, HI 96754

pages 97, 103 right
Gary Wolf Architects, Inc.
Boston, MA
(617) 742-7557

page 102
Tom Callaway
2920 Nebraska Ave.
Santa Monica, CA 90404

pages 104 right, 107 left
Karen Sugarman Interior Design
Andover, MA
(508) 475-2930

pages 114, 116
Alice Fellows
718 Copland Ct.
Santa Monica, CA 90291

page 118
Carla Schrad
9725 Green Oak Dr.
Los Angeles, CA 90068

Index

Photo Credits

William Abranowicz/
A+C Anthology: 119

©Kelly Bugden: pp. 57,
61 right

Courtesy of Crate&Barrel:
p. 74 right

©Philip Ennis: pp. 14, 28,
33 left, 35 left, 45, 59, 69
top, 70, 99, 105-106, 108
bottom, 109

©Michael Garland: pp. 7, 43
both (Design by Chris
Barrett), 51 (Design by
Judy Kenyon), 52 (Design
by Dan McGilvrey),
53 left (Architecture by
M. Lewis), 64, 81 (Design
by Joe Ruggeno),
83 (Design By Chris
Barrett), 90 and 94 top
(Design by Maxine
Ordesky), 94 bottom
(Design by Kelsey
Maddox-Bell), 114, 116
(Design by Alice Fellows),
118 (Design by Carla
Schrad)

©Tria Giovan: pp. 18, 22
and 24 (Design by
Patricia O'Shaughnessy),
26, 31, 37, 44 top
(Design by Michael
Foster), 44 bottom
(Design by Jody
Thompson Kennedy),
48, 58 bottom, 68, 73,
75, 80 right, 82 right
(Design by Tom Sansone),
85, 92, 93 (Patricia
O'Shaughnessy), 98
bottom, 101, 103 left
(Jody Thompson Kennedy)

©Nancy Hill: pp. 13, 33
right (Design by Kitchens
by Deane), 58 top, 71, 76
(Design by Ceman
Design), 77 (Design by
Kitchens by Krenzel,
St. Paul, MN), 95

©John Kane: pp. 11, 16, 56
bottom, 69 bottom, 82
left, 107 right

©image/Dennis Krukowski:
pp. 23 (Architecture by
Robert A. M. Stern),
74 left (Design by Mark
Zeff Consulting Group,
Inc.), 89 (Design by
George Constant, Inc.)

©David Livingston: pp. 54
left, 62 right

Courtesy of Luminaire,
Chicago: pp. 15, 17, 35
right, 60

©Eric Roth: pp. 9 (Design by
Anne Lenox-Partners in
Design, Newton Center,
MA), 21 (Design by Gayle
Reynolds, ASID, Lexington,
MA), 29 (Architecture by
Warner + Cunningham
Architects, Brookline,
MA), 34, 38 (Design by
Carole Kaplan-Two By
Two Interior Design,
Andover, MA), 42 (Design
by P.J. Wheeler Assoc.,
Boston), 49 right (Carole
Kaplan-Two By Two),
53 right (Design by
Beverly Payeff, Brookline,
NH), 54 right (Design by
Ericson Antique Stoves,
Littleton, MA), 56 top

(Design by Berg Howland
Assoc., Cambridge, MA),
65 left (Architecture by
Theodore & Theodore),
66 right, 79 (Carole
Kaplan-Two By Two),
84 (Design by Susan
Armstrong Interior
Design, Concord, MA),
88 (Carole Kaplan-Two
By Two), 97, 103 right
(Architecture by Gary
Wolf Architects, Inc,
Boston), 104 left (Anne
Lenox-Partners in
Design), 104 right, 107
left (Design by Karen
Sugarman Interior
Design, Andover, MA),
122 right

Eric Roth: ©David
Henderson: pp. 49 left
(Design by Debby Smith,
Nantucket, MA), 61 left,
62 left, 108 top

©Tim Street-Porter: pp.19,
30 (Design by Frank
Israel), 36 (Art/Design by
Annie Kelly), 78 (Design
by Shawn Stussy), 100
(Design by Mario
Tamayo), 102 (Design by
Tom Callaway), 122 left
(Design by Josseph
Terrell)

©Brian Vanden Brink: pp. 2
(Architecture by Jim
Sterling), 3, 5, 10 (Design
by Jane Langmuir,
Providence, RI), 12
(Architecture by
Centerbrook Architects),
25, 32, 39 (Architecture
by John Martin, Building

by Bullock & Co.),
40 (Building by Tom
Hampson), 46
(Architecture by Jim
Sterling), 50, 55, 63, 67,
86-87 (Architecture by
John Scholz), 91, 98 top
and 110 (Cabinet by
Duane Paluska), 113,
115, 121, 123 (Design by
Robert Currie)

©Dominique Vorillon:
pp. 41 (Architecture by
Daly-Genik), 65 right,
66 left (Design by Killory)

Front Jacket Photography:
©Tim Street-Porter
(Design by Jeffrey Tohl-
bottom)

Back Jacket Photography:
©Steve Gross & Susan
Daly (top); ©Brian
Vanden Brink (Design by
Centerbrook Architects)